HEDGEHOG CARE FOR BEGINNERS

A COMPREHENSIVE GUIDE ON HOW TO CARE, FEED, TRAIN, GROOM, HEALTH, HOUSE HEDGEHOG AND GUIDELINES TO RAISING THEM AS PETS

GARRY FREDICK

Made with ❤ on the Notion Press Platform
www.notionpress.com

Contents

Title Page

HEDGEHOG CARE FOR BEGINNERS

A comprehensive guide on how to care, feed, train, groom, health, house hedgehog and guidelines to raising them as pets

Garry Fredick

CHAPTER ONE

INTRODUCTION TO HEDGEHOGS

Pet hedgehogs have become quite famous in recent years, and as it should be. In spite of the fact that they aren't the cuddly sort of pet (because of their spiked exterior), these charming critters are fun and offer an alternate sort of satisfying experience of keeping pets.

The Natural History of Hedgehogs

Enter Caption

It's known to start in regions of Europe, Asia, and Africa, hedgehogs got their name from what they look like and where they like to hang out. Their nose looks like that of a pig, or a hog, and they're frequently found in the fences of bushes and trees.

Hedgehogs are warm blooded animals from the subfamily Erinaceinae. On account of their sharp defensive layer (armor), hedgehogs are regularly thought to be a far cousin of the porcupine. In any case, this misinterpretation is a long way from reality as porcupines are essentially rodents!

CHAPTER TWO

HEDGEHOGS AS HOUSE PETS

It is known from history that the ancient Romans were the first to train hedgehogs. In any case, the advanced taming of hedgehogs just took off during the 1980s. Numerous types of hedgehogs today are hybrids, the most notable being the African dwarf hedgehog.

The lifespan of the African dwarf hedgehog is is between 4 - 6 years all things considered, with good care, healthy and friendly environments.

Hedgehogs are prohibited in certain states, so before you settle on your choice on whether to bring one home, make certain to look at your state's laws on animals before you end up in great disappointment to you and your family.

Regular Breeds of Hedgehogs

The most widely recognized type of hedgehogs is the African dwarf hedgehog, additionally called the four-toed hedgehog or the white bellied hedgehog. They are for the most part between 6" - 8" long, making them an incredible pet for a little family unit. Other famous pet varieties are the European hedgehog and the long-eared hedgehog.

Where Should You Get Your Hedgehog?

After you have ensured that hedgehogs are allowed in your state, it is in every case best to go to a legitimate and honest breeder. At times it can happen that bigger pet chains do not convey exotic pets like hedgehogs, so it very well may be a smart thought to look at the more modest, specialty pet stores first.

CHAPTER THREE

HOW TO CARE FOR YOUR PET HEDGEHOG

Hedgehog Housing and climate

Enormous terrariums or strong base guinea pig confines make great lodging for hedgehogs. Since they like to explore the enclosure ought to be huge in size, 4‘ x2’. A bigger size confine additionally has better ventilation. C and C cages or enclosures are options that are pocket friendly and can be fabricated to be big enough for your hedgehog to roam about. Just strong base enclosures are appropriate for hedgehogs, any wire base cages could trap their legs or sham toenails. Give a delicate sheet material that doesn't contain dust, for example, reused paper pellets or in the event that you use wood shavings utilize just kiln dried pine or aspen. Try not to utilize cedar shavings as they cause irritation to your hedgehog's lungs. A few group give an extremely shallow litter box for their hedgehog (find it in the spot of the enclosure he likes to soil) fill it with a delicate pellet type litter or paper towels. Try not to utilize dirt or amassing cat litter.

For work out, notwithstanding an enclosure that is big enough, make a wheel accessible (additionally strong base without spokes to maintain a strategic distance from injury) that is huge enough for your hedgehog to use, there are some gigantic size ones made for chinchillas that would make great choices for your hedgehog. Give a spot to your hedgehog to shroud like a resting or sleeping pouch or igloo. Hedgehogs need natural temperatures somewhere in the range of 70 and 80 degrees. Get your hedgehog's confine far from drafts, direct daylight, or cold zones. You might need to give your hedgehog a little warm spot in his confine where he can go to get warm yet would likewise have the option to move away from on the off chance that he feels excessively warm. Check the reptile part of a pet store for different options accessible.

Hedgehogs are lone animals and should be housed alone. Male hedgehogs specifically will battle to death whenever housed together. To delight your hedgehog you can buy an assortment of cat or little toys for dogs. Simply ensure they don't have little regions where they can get their feet, nails, or noses caught.

Enter Caption

Hedgehog Enclosure Accessories

Ensure your confine has sufficient space for an exercise wheel and also a spot big enough for your hedgehog to hide when the need arises for it to sleep. This concealing spot can be nearly anything, from a cardboard box to something you find at the pet store.

The exercise wheel is a vital piece of keeping up your hedgehog's health and wellbeing. Without sufficient opportunity to go around in and outside of their enclosure, your hedgehog is in danger of getting overweight. Truth be told, excessive fatness is unfortunately very normal among hedgehogs. Ensure the wheel is strong, and not made of wire; their feet can stall out in the wires and this may cause cracked appendages. In a perfect world the wheel ought to associate with 11" to 12" in breadth.

We likewise urge you to give your hedgehogs toys to keep them entertained and active at the same time. You can put an assortment of toys into the pen and see what they like. A few top picks are cylinders and balls with ringers (like the ones for cats).

Hedgehog Enclosure Temperatures

Another significant part of your hedgehog's house is keeping up the correct temperature. Hedgehogs feel best in temperatures between 75 - 85 degrees Fahrenheit. Temperatures that are too hot or too cold can make a hedgehog dormant. Cold temperatures can make your hedgehog endeavor to hibernate, which can be lethal in bondage. On the off chance that the temperatures do drop, slowly raise the temperature, and utilize an aberrant warming cushion to help bit by bit warm up your hedgehog. The best strategy is to hold your hedgehog against your skin. When it seems like your hedgehog has returned to an ordinary temperature, carry your hedgehog to the vet.

During the colder months, a straightforward method to keep up the right temperature is by utilizing an outside warming source, for example, a warmth light like the ones regularly utilized for reptiles. On the off chance that you decide to set up a heater or a warmth bulb, ensure there are numerous thermometers so you can check the warmth.

CHAPTER FOUR

HEDGEHOG DIET AND NUTRITION

What Do Hedgehogs Eat?

In the wild, a hedgehog's eating regimens comprise of bugs, plants, and roots. This eating routine is difficult to repeat in confinement. The most adjusted eating routine for your pet hedgehog is a combination of dry food, live enhancements or supplements, and treats.

There are food combinations made explicitly for hedgehogs, however they are frequently difficult to track down. No compelling reason to stress, there are different alternatives that are comparable. Ensure that the base food is a combination of 2 - 3 various types of meat-rich, dry cat food, with a fat substance under 10% (if conceivable). Fish can cause problems for African pygmies or dwarfs, so it's prescribed to stay with chicken flavor.

Live food is a decent supplement for your hedgehog's eating routine. Crickets, cockroaches, and mealworms are a portion of their top picks. Different nourishments that can be given as intermittent treats incorporate mixed or bubbled eggs, peas, broccoli, apple, pounded potato, cooked sheep, chicken or mince, and dog food.

Water

Water ought to consistently be accessible for your hedgehog in its walled in area. Your hedgehog will drink water from a little bowl, which ought to be cleaned consistently. A few hedgehogs will drink from bottles. On the off chance that you are checking/trying to check whether your hedgehog will drink from a jug, make certain to incorporate a water bowl in the fenced in area during this time for testing until you are sure they are drinking from the container.

CHAPTER FIVE

HEDGEHOG BEHAVIOR

At the point when you initially get your hedgehog, it is imperative to get them used to being handled by you. Most hedgehogs will get familiar with your touch on the off chance that you handle them frequently, and are cautious with them. From the start, the normal intuition for hedgehogs is to twist into a ball. After some time, with enough persistence, your hedgehog will unwind, open up, and begin to crawl all around you.

The least demanding approach to make this process smoother is by getting your hedgehog when it is at a youthful age. From the start, you should allow your hedgehog to become accustomed to its new environmental factors, and maybe give it a couple of days with minimal touches. Gradually you will show your hedgehog to become accustomed to your fragrance, and afterward things will get simpler (so don't wear gloves.) Be mindful so as not to frighten your hedgehog; a surprised hedgehog may mess with you.

An odd however regular interaction called self-anointing may occur, where your hedgehog salivates intensely, spreads the spit everywhere on its back, and distorts into some abnormal positions. This cycle is normally set off by an odd smell. It isn't anything to stress over, and a few group even think that it's charming.

A sound hedgehog needs to go around and let off some pressure. After hedgehog-proofing your place, give your mate time to go around outside of the walled in area.

Hedgehogs are Nocturnal

Hedgehogs are known to sleep at day time and are awake and active at night. Since they start their movement at night, before you head to bed would be a decent an ideal opportunity to invest energy with and bond with your hedgehog.

The way of life of a nighttime pet may imply that you'll need to get your hedgehog's fenced in area far from your room, particularly in the event that you are quite sensitive to noise. Else it will keep you up the entire night running on its wheel or playing with its toys.

CHAPTER SIX

GROOMING YOUR HEDGEHOG

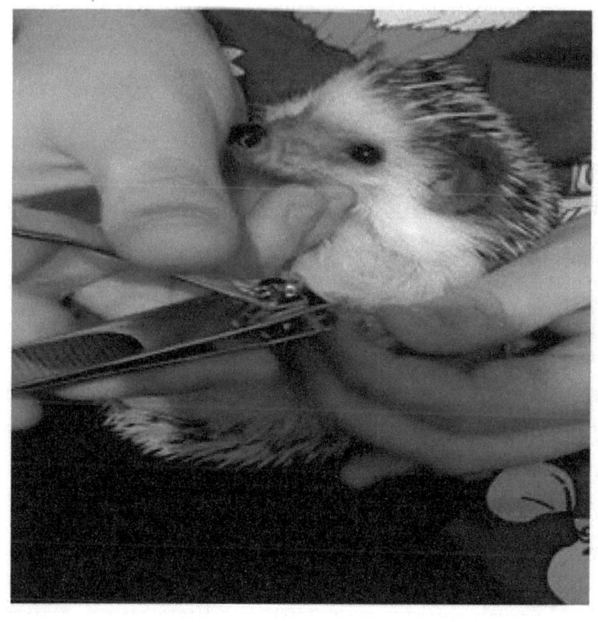

Enter Caption

Enter Caption

Ensure you trimthe nails of your hedgehog and bath them on a regular basis.

To cut your hedgehog's nails, hold the hedgehog on its back on your lab and delicately hold one of its paws. When the hedgehog is still, you nail trimmers to cute the white tip on the nail, ensure you do not cut the brisk. Steady trimmings shorten the quick and reduce the possibility of hurting your hedgehog. In the event that you end up scratching your hedgehog, use cornstarch to stop the bleeding as fast as you can.

When washing/bathing a hedgehog, fill a bath, sink, or little basin with tepid water. Utilize a little cup to wet your hedgehog, yet try not to get water in your hedgehog's ear to maintain a strategic distance from an ear contamination. Put a toothpaste estimated dot of hedgehog-friendly body wash on the toothbrush and brush similar way as the quills. Wash altogether and try to not give up any bubbles as these can aggravate and dry the skin. Use a towel to wrap the hedgehog to keep it warm until it dries toprevent any scares of it hibernating.

CHAPTER SEVEN

MEDICAL CARE FOR YOUR PET HEDGEHOG

To guarantee a sound life for your hedgehog, plan a yearly test with a dedicated exotic pet vet for an actual test that incorporates fecal and blood work.

After getting your hedgehog, you should go to your vet to analyze it for regular parasites like vermin.

Basic Hedgehog Health Concerns

Like people, hedgehogs can likewise gain comparative infections like greasy liver illness, cardiovascular sickness, and also cancer.

Liver sickness and excessive fatness (obesity) frequently happen as a result of unfortunate dietary patterns, an uneven eating routine, and lack of good exercise.

Balloon disorder or syndrome is an uncommon and abnormal state of hedgehogs. Gas gets caught under the skin, making the hedgehog explode like a balloon. This condition is interesting to hedgehogs originating from the manner in which their skin is fabricated. In the event that you notice that your pet hedgehog has balloon syndrome, carry them to your vet right away.

Female hedgehogs are likewise profoundly inclined to uterine tumors. We prescribed spaying all female hedgehogs to wipe out the danger of this deadly condition.

How to Tell When My Hedgehog Is Sick?

Below are some signs and symptoms to show that your hedgehog might be ill. Should you notice any of these signs, plan a meeting with your close by vet:

- Lethargy
- Flakes or crust on the skin, or losing spikes (might be an external parasite)
- Loss of Appetite
- Coughing, wheezing
- Diarrhea
- Weight loss
- Anemia
- excreting blood
- Wobbling/loss of command over their appendages
- Squealing while passing out urine
- Cloudy release from the nose
- Discoloration release from the ear

Printed by Libri Plureos GmbH in Hamburg,
Germany